4/14

WHEN pets ATTACK!

COYOTES AND WOLVES
ARE NOT PETS!

Gareth Stevens
Publishing

BY BARBARA LINDE

Dedication: For my writers group: Linda, Doris, Beverly, and Daria. Long may we critique!

Please visit our website, www.garethstevens.com. For a free color catalog of all our high-quality books, call toll free 1-800-542-2595 or fax 1-877-542-2596.

Library of Congress Cataloging-in-Publication Data

Linde, Barbara M.
Coyotes and wolves are not pets! / by Barbara M. Linde.
    p. cm. — (When pets attack)
Includes index.
ISBN 978-1-4339-9294-0 (pbk.)
ISBN 978-1-4339-9295-7 (6-pack)
ISBN 978-1-4339-9293-3 (library binding)
1. Coyote—Juvenile fiction. 2. Wolves—Juvenile literature. 3. Canidae—Juvenile literature. I. Linde, Barbara M. II. Title.
QL737.C22 L56 2014
599.77'3—dc23

First Edition

Published in 2014 by
Gareth Stevens Publishing
111 East 14th Street, Suite 349
New York, NY 10003

Copyright © 2014 Gareth Stevens Publishing

Designer: Katelyn E. Reynolds
Editor: Therese Shea

Photo credits: Cover, pp. 1, 4, 5 (both), 7, 22, 25 iStockphoto/Thinkstock.com; cover, pp. 1–32 (home sweet home image) © iStockphoto.com/DNY59; cover, pp. 1–32 (background) Hemera/Thinkstock.com; cover, pp. 1–32 (blood splatter), pp. 3–32 (frame) iStockphoto/Thinkstock.com; p. 9 Panoramic Images/ Getty Images; p. 11 (map) maplab/Wikipedia.com; p. 11 (image) Oldrich/Shutterstock.com; p. 13 (map) Tommyknocker/Wikipedia.com; p. 13 (image) Roy Toft/Oxford Scientific/Getty Images; p. 15 Ingrid Curry/ Shutterstock.com; p. 16 Jim Kruger/E+/Getty Images; p. 17 Comstock/Thinkstock.com; p. 19 Christina Krutz/ Radius Images/Getty Images; p. 20 Karen Grigoryan/Shutterstock.com; p. 21 Iiya D. Gridnev/Shutterstock.com; p. 23 L. Kragt Bakker/Shutterstock.com; p. 24 Bill Frische/Shutterstock.com; p. 27 Brenda Carson/Shutterstock.com; p. 28 Matt Knoth/Shutterstock.com; p. 29 Silvia Otte/Photodisc/Getty Images.

Printed in the United States of America

CPSIA compliance information: Batch #CS13GS: For further information contact Gareth Stevens, New York, New York at 1-800-542-2595.

CONTENTS

Meet the *Canis* Canines 4

Comparing Coyotes and Wolves 6

Family Life 8

Coyote Habitats 10

Wolf Habitats 12

Why Coyotes and Wolves Are Important 14

Pets Gone Wrong 18

Attacks 22

Protecting Yourself from an Attack 26

Coexisting 28

Glossary 30

For More Information 31

Index 32

Words in the glossary appear in **bold** type the first time they are used in the text.

MEET THE *CANIS* CANINES

Coyotes, wolves, and dogs are all members of the animal group *Canis*. About 15,000 years ago, some wolves became **domesticated**. Scientists think hungry wolves stayed near human settlements, eating scraps. Over time, these wolves became tame. People figured out how to train the wolves as helpers. The dogs we love as pets are the **descendants** of these animals.

Coyotes are related to both dogs and wolves. However, no matter how much your dog looks like a wolf or a coyote, only the dog is a pet. Wolves and coyotes are wild animals and shouldn't be in your home.

dog

bone STUDY

Scientists study the bones of ancient wolves and dogs. That's how they're able to figure out how and when dogs probably first became domesticated.

Dogs you see today haven't been around for long, though. The oldest dog breeds are no more than 500 years old, and most date only from about 150 years ago!

You can see the family resemblance by looking at a dog, wolf, and coyote side by side.

coyote

wolf

COMPARING COYOTES AND WOLVES

Dogs can vary in size from tiny teacup Yorkshire terriers to huge Irish wolfhounds. Coyotes and wolves are somewhere in between these. Use the chart to compare the two.

	GRAY WOLVES	COYOTES
LENGTH (nose to tail)	4.5 to 6.5 feet (1.4 to 2 m)	3.6 to 4.4 feet (1.1 to 1.3 m)
HEIGHT (at the shoulder)	26 to 32 inches (66 to 81 cm)	18 to 24 inches (46 to 61 cm)
WEIGHT	60 to 150 pounds (27 to 68 kg)	20 to 50 pounds (9 to 23 kg)
COAT	gray, black, or white	yellow, gray, or brownish with black tips
EARS	short, rounded	long, pointed
MUZZLE (nose and jaws)	large, square	small, pointed
TOP SPEED	38 miles (61 km) per hour	40 miles (64 km) per hour

what's on THE MENU?

Coyotes and wolves are **omnivores**. They eat small animals, such as birds, snakes, and mice. They chow down on just about anything from fruits and vegetables to grass and flowers. But they also hunt large animals, such as elk, deer, and moose. They eat a lot at one time if they can. They may go days before eating again.

7

FAMILY LIFE

Wolves and coyotes live in packs. They form male and female pairs when it's time to mate. They often stay together for life. The animals build a dry, cozy den in a cave, under the ground, in a log, or in another sheltered spot. A female coyote may have as many as six pups at a time. A female wolf has as many as 11 pups.

The whole pack takes care of the pups. The pups drink their mothers' milk until they're old enough to eat food. That's about 3 weeks for a wolf and about 6 weeks for a coyote.

HOWL!

Coyotes and wolves howl for many reasons. They howl to greet other members of the pack. They howl to call the pack together to hunt. They howl extra loud to warn other animals to stay away. If you think your dog makes a lot of noise, that's nothing compared to a coyote or wolf!

In the wild, wolves and coyotes live up to 14 years. In protected parks or zoos, they may live up to 20 years.

COYOTE HABITATS

Originally, the coyote lived in western North America. One of their main predators was the wolf. As people began settling these areas, they killed many wolves. As a result, the number of coyotes increased, and they took over wolf **habitats**.

When these areas got crowded, coyotes moved eastward. The wolves in the East had already died out. Coyotes easily **adapt** to new surroundings, so the move was successful. Now, their **range** includes the United States, from West Coast to East Coast, as well as Canada and Mexico.

coyote TALES

Coyotes were important to the Native American people. They appear often in Native American tales. Coyotes are tricksters who try to fool people or other animals. They're often outwitted, however. In some tales, the coyote is the creature that made the first people.

Coyote Range Map

North America

☐ coyote territory

Scientists believe that coyotes first arrived in New York in the 1920s.

WOLF HABITATS

Wolves used to live across most of North America, Europe, and Asia. It's thought that at one time, there were almost 2 million wolves on Earth. People have long feared wolves, because they're so fierce. Over time, people hunted them until they became **endangered** and nearly **extinct**. Laws had to be made to protect them.

Now, there are about 200,000 wolves worldwide. Many of them live in Canada or Asia. As many as 11,000 wolves may live in Alaska, with another 5,000 in Idaho, Michigan, Minnesota, Montana, Wisconsin, and Wyoming.

wolf TALES

Wolves are often the evil characters in fairy tales. Think about "The Three Little Pigs" or "Little Red Riding Hood." However, wolves are heroes in other stories. In Roman myths, a wolf raised two boys named Romulus and Remus. They were the children of the god Mars, and they later founded the city of Rome.

Wolf Range Map

North America

Europe

Asia

Africa

present wolves
past wolves

Wolves need a lot of open space to roam.

WHY COYOTES AND WOLVES ARE IMPORTANT

Wolves and coyotes are needed in their habitats because of their important role in nature. Coyotes are even useful to people in cities and towns. They eat rats, bugs, and birds, so they help control these populations. Farmers and gardeners are often happy to have coyotes dine on weasels, moles, and other pests. When coyotes have eaten their fill, smaller animals move in and eat the leftovers.

Coyotes also eat old and **diseased** animals. Removing these animals helps the rest of the population and the whole habitat. Without coyotes, some animal populations might grow too large and upset the balance of the habitat.

protection LAWS

Federal laws once protected wolves and helped their population bounce back. Now there are no federal laws protecting wolves or coyotes. Some states protect the animals from hunters and trappers, but others don't. No one knows yet how these changes will affect the wolf and coyote populations in the future.

This coyote in an Arizona desert may have its eyes on a tasty meal.

Nearly 500 wolves now live in Yellowstone National Park.

Wolves, too, play an important role in their habitats. Long ago, wolves roamed freely in Yellowstone National Park in Wyoming. As more people visited and hunted in the park, the wolves were killed off. Because wolves eat elk and coyotes, the populations of those animals got larger. There wasn't enough food for them, and many starved. The elk also damaged numerous trees and plants.

Wolves were put back into Yellowstone in 1995. Elk and coyote numbers went down. Up to 20 other animals and birds eat wolves' leftovers, so there was more food for these animals, too.

Visitors to Yellowstone can drive or walk through parts of the park where they can see wolves. There are rules about how far away visitors should stay. Some of the wolves wear radio collars, so wildlife experts can keep track of them. They share the information they gather with visitors.

PETS GONE WRONG

Some people raise coyote or wolf pups. This isn't a good idea. No matter how cute and cuddly the pups are, they're still wild animals. When they grow to be adults, their **instincts** take over. They fight to become the **dominant** member of the pack—and they may fight you!

Wild canines are hard to train. It takes lots of time and effort to do even a little bit of training, and you can never be sure if they'll continue to obey you. They also mark their territory. They leave their waste to warn off other animals. You don't want them doing this in your house!

what the EXPERTS SAY

Many groups are against owning wild animals as pets, including the American Veterinary Medicine Association, the National Animal Control Association, and the American Zoo and Aquarium Association. They think it's dangerous for people to try to control the animals. It's also unhealthy—and even cruel—for the wild animals.

It took thousands of years for dogs to become suitable pets for people. A single lifetime probably isn't enough for a wolf or coyote, even if they're raised by people their whole life.

You don't want a pet to end up living like this!

Just like regular pets, coyotes and wolves may get sick or carry diseases. Unlike your dog or cat, however, many veterinarians won't treat wild animals. In some states, it's against the law for them to do so!

Your hungry pet needs to eat, and remember that coyotes and wolves eat meat. Where will you get all the fresh food your wild pet wants?

Coyotes and wolves are used to living in packs, not alone or with a person. They're also outdoor animals. They won't want to stay in your house. Even if you have a huge backyard, they'll feel cramped. And they may even try to attack other pets—or even people!

volunteer!

If you really want to be around wild animals, **volunteer** at a local wildlife park or shelter. Many of these places raise injured wild animals or those that have been dropped off by people who can't take care of them anymore. You can be helpful to those poor animals and learn a lot about them, too.

ATTACKS

Since 1942, there have been about 50 wolf attacks in North America. Three people died of rabies. In 2005 and 2010, two people died from the injuries they received in the attacks.

Coyotes have attacked at least 160 people in the United States in the past 30 years. Two people have died from coyote attacks—a 3-year old girl who was attacked in her driveway and a 19-year-old female hiker. Coyotes seem to attack young, small children the most. This is another important reason *not* to have a coyote as a pet.

rabies

Rabies is a disease that can kill animals and people. A person can get rabies if bitten or scratched by an animal that has rabies. If the person gets medicine in time and if the injuries aren't too severe, the person will recover. Some people who work around animals get rabies shots to prevent the disease.

Do not feed the coyotes.

Feeding wild coyotes and wolves only encourages them to get closer to people, which can result in attacks.

Some places have "wolf caution areas," so that hunters and hikers will be extra careful.

traveling **BY TRAIN**

In 2006, a coyote that had rabies tried to get into a house in Reading, Pennsylvania. The homeowners' two dogs battled the coyote until the homeowners killed it.

In February 2002, a coyote walked through an open train door at the Portland International Airport—and took a seat! Luckily, no riders were on the train. An airport wildlife specialist captured the animal. He moved it to a wilderness area beyond the airport.

In June 2012, a zoo worker in Sweden was attacked and killed by wolves. She had entered a cage with eight wolves alone, as she had done since they were pups. No one is exactly sure what happened.

In December 2012, three coyotes attacked a man and his dog in his backyard in Washington State. Although the man was scratched and bitten, he finally shook off the coyotes. He got several rabies shots afterwards.

PROTECTING YOURSELF FROM AN ATTACK

You'll probably never be attacked by a wolf. Since coyotes live closer to people, an attack is more possible, although still not likely. With both animals, be safe, and know what to do.

First, never walk alone in a wild area. A group of people is **intimidating** to wild animals. If you're alone and see a coyote or wolf, don't run. Stand your ground. Then, yell, wave your arms, and try to look scary. You can even throw sticks and rocks. If they still approach, try punching them on the nose. If all else fails, climb a tree and wait for help.

fight the urge TO FLEE

Never run away from an attacking coyote or wolf. Coyotes and wolves are more likely to attack someone if they're running away. This is what their other prey does. Remember, these predators are expert hunters. They'll chase you, and they're much faster than the fastest person.

COEXISTING

In Denver, Colorado, coyotes had been seen frequently at a park in the morning, when people were walking their dogs. Some pets had been hurt or killed, and people were scared. Park staff came up with a plan for coyotes and people to coexist, or live peacefully in the same areas. It's called hazing.

Trained wildlife workers went to the park every morning at the same time. They banged pots, blew whistles, and made a lot of noise. After a few weeks, the coyotes stopped coming to the park in the morning. The workers trained the local people in their hazing methods.

remember!

There have been recent coyote sightings in large cities like Los Angeles, California; Chicago, Illinois; and New York City. With the amount of food available in these places, coyotes may be people's neighbors for a long time. Coexistence is not the same thing as having a wild animal as a pet. That is never, ever, a wise choice.

Always keep your distance from wolves and coyotes.

You never know when they'll attack.

GLOSSARY

adapt: to change to suit new conditions

descendant: an animal that comes from an animal of an earlier time

diseased: having an illness

domesticate: to raise an animal so it can live with or be used by people

dominant: the most powerful or strongest

endangered: in danger of dying out

extinct: no longer living

federal: relating to the national government

habitat: the natural place where an animal or plant lives

instinct: an inborn reaction or behavior that aids in survival

intimidate: to create a feeling of fear or awe in a person or animal

omnivore: an animal that eats both plants and animals

range: the area where something lives

volunteer: a person who works without being paid

FOR MORE INFORMATION

Books

Read, Tracy C. *Exploring the World of Coyotes.* Buffalo, NY: Firefly Books, 2011.

Tekiela, Stan. *The Lives of Wolves, Coyotes, and Foxes.* Cambridge, MN: Adventure Publications, 2012.

Websites

Coyote
animals.howstuffworks.com/mammals/coyote-info.htm
Get the facts about coyotes.

Coyote
animals.nationalgeographic.com/animals/mammals/coyote/
Hear what a coyote sounds like.

In the Valley of the Wolves
www.pbs.org/wnet/nature/episodes/in-the-valley-of-the-wolves/video-full-episode/4678/
This PBS video tells the story of a Yellowstone wolf pack.

INDEX

Asia 12

attacks 21, 22, 23, 25, 26, 27, 29

Canada 10, 12

Canis 4

coexisting 28

den 8

diseases 21, 22

dogs 4, 5, 6, 8, 19, 21, 25, 28

domesticated 4

Europe 12

fairy tales 12

habitats 10, 12, 14, 17

hazing 28

howling 8

hunting 6, 8

instincts 18

laws 12, 14, 21

Mexico 10

myths 12

Native Americans 10

North America 10, 12, 22

omnivores 6

packs 8, 18, 21

parks 9, 21, 28

pups 8, 18, 25

rabies 22, 25

range 10, 11, 13

safety 26

size 6

tracks 7

training 4, 18

United States 10, 22

Yellowstone National Park 16, 17

zoos 9, 25